Making Masks

Helen and Peter McNiven

With photographs by Chris Fairclough

Thomson Learning • New York

FIRST ARTS & CRAFTS

Books in this series

Collage
Drawing
Making Masks
Models
Painting
Printing
Puppets
Toys and Games

For Sophie

First published in the
United States in 1995 by
Thomson Learning
115 Fifth Avenue
New York, NY 10003

First published in Great Britain in 1994 by Wayland (Publishers) Ltd.

Library of Congress Cataloging-in-Publication Data
McNiven, Helen and Peter
 Making masks/Helen and Peter McNiven; with photographs
by Chris Fairclough.
    p.   cm.—(First arts & crafts)
 Includes bibliographical references and index.
 ISBN 1-56847-212-9
 1. Mask making—Juvenile literature. 2. Papier mâché—Juvenile
literature. [1. Mask making. 2. Masks. 3. Handicraft.]
I. McNiven, Peter (Peter Alister) II. Fairclough, Chris, ill. III. Title.
IV. Series.
TT898.M36   1994
731'.75—dc20   94-22080

Printed in Italy

Contents

Making masks 4

Painted faces 6

Picture glasses 8

Mosaic faces 10

Cartoon characters 12

Self-portraits 14

Modeling with dough 16

Animals 18

Pecking birds 20

Hiding in the rain forest 22

Wild beasts 24

Front and side 26

Chinese dragons 28

Helpful hints 30

Glossary 31

Further information 32

Index 32

Making masks

A mask is a face people hide behind. With a mask, anyone can become someone or something different. Masks are mysterious.

People have made masks throughout history. Cave people wore masks to help them feel brave when they went hunting. The ancient Egyptians and many other peoples believed masks could protect them from evil.

Tassili rock painting, Algeria.

Kenyan tribal mask.

Actors have used masks to make them look like other people. This began in Greek and Roman times. Then people started wearing masks at festivals and dances. Today, we still wear masks for fun and at parties.

The masks in this book are easy to make from everyday things. You can find most of them at home or school. Ask an adult to help you gather what you need. Make sure you read through each project carefully before you start making a mask.

Ask an adult to help you when you cut things. You'll be using a knife or a hole punch to make holes to see through. Eye holes should be about a quarter of an inch wide and about 2¾ inches apart.

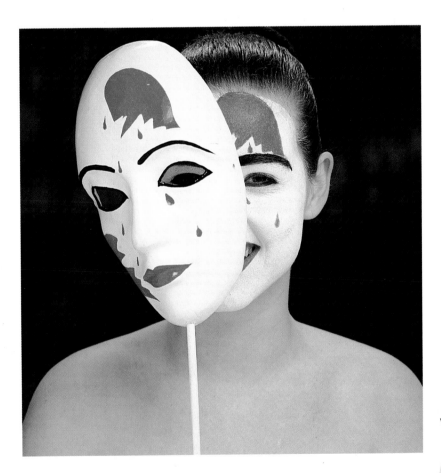

Masks by Geoff Redmayne.

Each mask here is a beginning. You can add more textures, patterns, and colors. Add as many as you wish. Your masks don't have to look like these – they will be much more fun if they don't!

Painted faces

The simplest mask is a painted face.

People paint their faces for many different reasons: for religious festivals, carnivals, camouflage, or just for fun. One of the best known painted faces is a clown face.

You will need:

A mirror

Nontoxic face paints

Brightly colored, thick yarn

Scissors

Rubber band

Look in the mirror and make some funny faces. What happens to your mouth if you look sad?

With your face paints, draw a short line straight up above each eye. Then draw another line down below each eye. Be careful not to get paint in your eyes.

Now draw lines from your eye corners. Move your eyes from side to side.

Paint your face in different ways. Paint your lips bigger than they are. Paint the lines and shapes in your face, like the curve of your eyebrows or the shape of your cheeks.

See how different colors make your face look. Try light and dark colors.

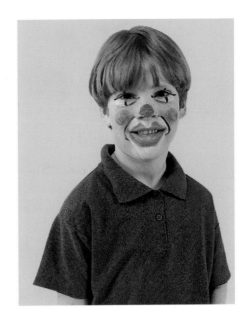

Add a mop of hair. Cut lots of yarn into 2-foot lengths. Lay the strands together and tie them in the middle with a rubber band. Put the yarn on your head, with the strands falling down around your face.

7

Picture glasses

Look at your family, friends, and other people around you. Everyone's face is different. Look at photographs of different faces in magazines.

You will need:
Magazines
Scissors
Cardboard
Pencil
White glue
Felt-tipped pens or paints
Hole punch

Look through magazines and cut out some big eyes. You can use these to make a pair of glasses.

● On a large piece of cardboard, draw the shape of a pair of glasses. The arms will bend back and sit over your ears. You could draw carefully around a pair of glasses first to get the shape you need.

Cut out the glasses from the cardboard.
Glue some big eyes behind the frames of
the glasses, so that they can be seen from
the front.
Make small holes in the center of the eyes
so that you can see through them.
Now, bend the arms back and put your
glasses on.

You can add patterns and colors with
felt-tipped pens or paints. Make your
glasses as big and as funny as you like.
You could add a nose and mouth, too.

Mosaic faces

A long time ago, artists started making pictures and patterns like this on floors and walls. They used small pieces of colored stone. This technique is called mosaic. People still make mosaics today.

You will need:

Cardboard or a plain
paper plate

Magazines

Scissors

Pencil

Glue

Hole punch or knife

Elastic

Mosaic faces of Mary with Jesus, from the Kykko monastery in Cyprus.

Eastern Nigerian mask decorated with beads and shells.

You can make a mosaic mask. Think about the colors you want to use. Tear or cut out one-inch chunks of different colors from magazines. You could collect skin colors, very bright colors, or different parts of faces, such as noses, eyes, and mouths.

Cut a paper plate or a piece of plain cardboard into a face shape about 8½ inches long by 7 inches wide. Draw lightly on your shape where you want the eyes, nose, and mouth to be. Glue pieces of ripped magazine paper onto your mask to make a lively, colorful face. Rip the pieces smaller if you need to.

- Make holes for your eyes.
- Make a small hole on each side of your mask, in line with the eyes.
- Push one end of the elastic through one hole from the back of the mask to the front. Make a knot in the end of the elastic so that it cannot pull through the hole.
- Do the same with the other end of the elastic on the other side of the mask.

Cartoon characters

Look at these children's drawings of cartoon characters. What makes each character look different from any other? One might wear a colorful hat. Another might have a round nose or funny hair.

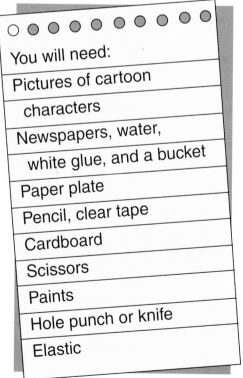

You will need:

Pictures of cartoon
  characters
Newspapers, water,
  white glue, and a bucket
Paper plate
Pencil, clear tape
Cardboard
Scissors
Paints
Hole punch or knife
Elastic

Let's make a mask of your favorite cartoon character. So far in this book you have made masks that are flat. Now build up the shape of a face using cardboard or papier-mâché, which is a sort of mushy paper.

Papier-mâché is made like this (ask an adult to help you):

● Tear up newspaper into lots of small squares.
● Put the newspaper pieces into a bucket and cover with warm water.

Let stand for a few hours until the newspaper is soaking wet. Pour the water out, leaving the wet newspaper behind. Using your hands, mix enough white glue into the wet newspaper to make it soft and sticky.

Now make your mask.

Draw the face of your character on a paper plate. Make holes for your eyes. Add things like hats by gluing or taping on extra pieces of cardboard.

- Build up the cheeks, eyebrows, and nose by adding more pieces of cardboard and wet papier-mâché pulp.
- Let your mask dry for at least two days.
- Paint it to look like your cartoon character. Add elastic as you did on page 11.

Self-portraits

We all look different because our faces are different shapes and colors.

You will need:

A blown-up balloon

Newspapers

A paste of flour, warm
   water, and white glue

Pin

Hole punch and knife

Pencil, mirror

Papier-mâché pulp
   (see page 12)

Paints

Elastic

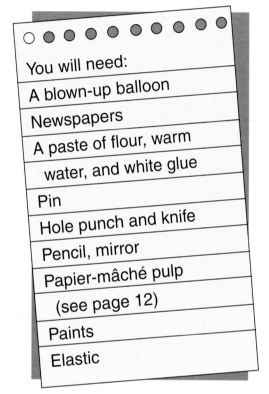

With this mask you make your own face. It is called a self-portrait.

Faces are not flat. They are rounded. That is why you start to make this mask on a blown-up balloon. This project uses another method of papier-mâché called layering.

- Tear up some old newspaper into lots of small pieces.
- Ask an adult to help you mix some flour, warm water, and white glue into a paste.
- Dip the newspaper pieces into the paste and cover the balloon with four layers.

After the newspaper has dried for at least a day, pop the balloon with a pin. Ask an adult to help you cut your newspaper balloon in half with a knife. Now you have the start of two masks. On one, sketch in the eyes, nose, and mouth, and cut holes for your eyes.

Look at your face in a mirror. Which parts of your face stick out? Which are curved or flat?

Now build up the face on your mask with papier-mâché pulp made from the recipe on page 12.

When you have finished, let your self-portrait dry. Then paint it, looking at all the different colors in your face. Add elastic (see page 11) so that you can wear it.

Modeling with dough

Some masks are made by carving shapes and lines out of wood. Many masks are made by modeling something when it is soft, like clay or papier-mâché, then letting it dry until it is hard.

You will need:

3 cups plain flour

1 cup salt

Water

Rolling pin and more flour

A blunt knife

Paints and varnish

A Tlingit tribal mask of wood, fiber, and feathers, Pacific Northwest.

You can also model a mask using a soft bread dough. Ask an adult to help you.

Mix the flour and salt with about 1½ cups of water. The mixture should become like soft modeling compound. Press out some dough, about half an inch thick, on a flat work top. Make a big face shape. Cover the work top with flour so that your dough does not stick. Now make faces in the dough.

Do not eat this dough.

You can use a blunt knife to make lines. Model shapes by squeezing and pulling the dough with your fingers. Ask an adult to help you bake your mask. Put it in a warm oven at 250 degrees for about an hour and a half, until it is dry but not brown. When your mask is cool, you can paint it. Varnish will make the mask very shiny.

Add all sorts of other things to make your mask exciting. Glue on feathers, shells, or beads. Make holes in the mask and push string, yarn, or rags through. Hang up your finished mask.

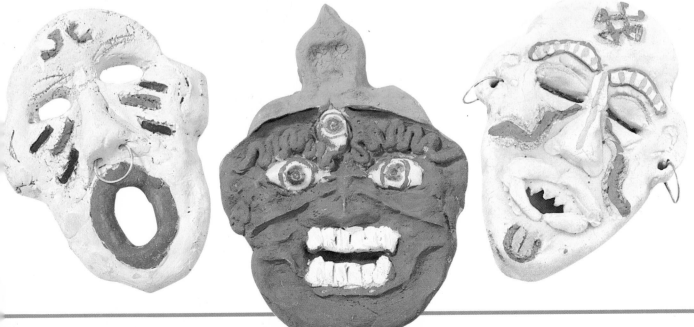

Animals

Animal faces make wonderful masks. Look at pictures of animals. Think of all the different masks you could make. You can make masks of real animals or think up your own wild creatures.

You will need:

Empty cereal box or
  plain cardboard

Pencil

Scissors

Glue

Paints

A variety of things to glue
  on your masks, such as
  feathers, yarn, and fabric

Hole punch or knife

Elastic

● Ask an adult to help you cut off the back of a cereal box. Copy the lines from the picture below onto the piece of box or a plain piece of cardboard. The dotted lines are where you will fold the cardboard. Cut along the blue lines.

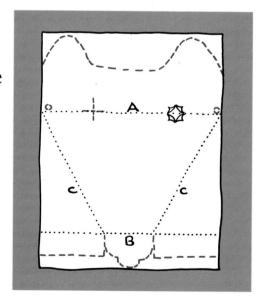

Make the eyes by cutting two crosses like those in the picture. Then fold out each of the four points.

Now fold the top part of the cardboard along line A so that it sticks up.

Fold the bottom part of the cardboard along line B so that it points down.

Fold the sides down along the lines marked C to make a long nose. Glue the flaps of cardboard under the end of the nose.

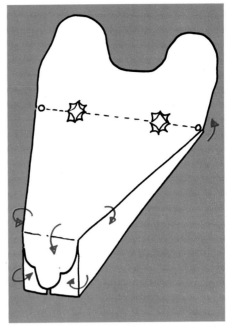

Use paints or collect things such as feathers, string, strips of colored paper, fabric, and yarn to make interesting animal markings.

Add some elastic, as you did on page 11, and put on your mask.

Pecking birds

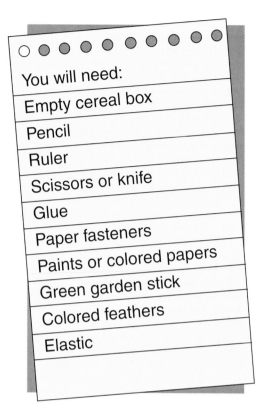

You will need:

Empty cereal box

Pencil

Ruler

Scissors or knife

Glue

Paper fasteners

Paints or colored papers

Green garden stick

Colored feathers

Elastic

Native Americans used to make bird masks that they held up on sticks when they danced. They could also make the birds' beaks move.

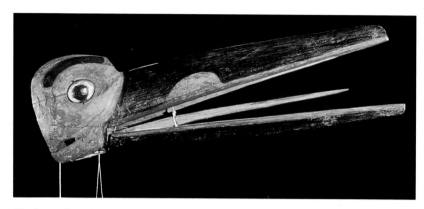

Nishga bird mask, Pacific Northwest.

Ask an adult to help you make a bird mask with a beak that moves. Look at the diagrams carefully.

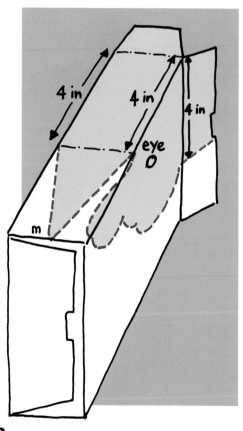

- You will use all of a cereal box.
- Measure down 4 inches at each corner of one long, narrow side. Make a mark at the middle of the bottom edge (m), and draw lines to the 4-inch marks to the m to make a "V"-shaped tongue.
- Now draw your bird's head shape on both sides of the box (copy the shape from the picture on the left). Cut out the head and tongue (the shaded area). Make an eyehole on either side.

Flatten out the rest of the box. Measure the width of the side panel (x) along the top of the front (A) and at the bottom of the back (B). Now draw lines as shown in the picture. Cut out the beaks by following these blue lines.
Stick the upper beak above the "V"-shaped tongue on your mask.
Slide the lower beak in under the tongue and attach with paper fasteners. Glue on a stick to make your beak open and close.

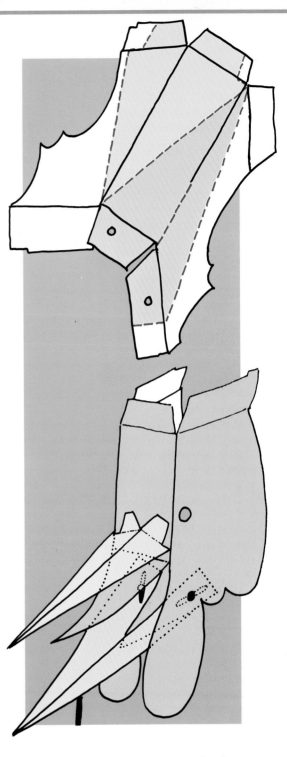

Glue or paint brightly colored feathers onto your mask. Add some elastic (see page 11) so you can wear it.

Hiding in the rain forest

Look at this painting of animals in a rain forest. Some of the animals are hiding behind trees and leafy plants.

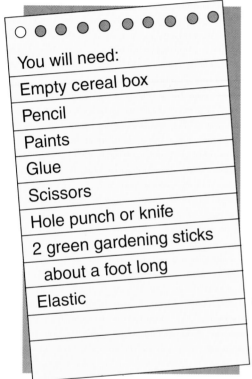

You will need:

Empty cereal box

Pencil

Paints

Glue

Scissors

Hole punch or knife

2 green gardening sticks about a foot long

Elastic

Part of *The Dream* by Henri Rousseau (1844-1910).

You can make a mask that hides behind another mask.

- Draw and paint big leaf shapes filling the front of the cereal box.
- Cut two "doors" as shown. This is the front mask, which hides another mask behind it.
- Open the doors. On the back of the box draw and make an animal mask as you did before (see pages 18-19). Add elastic as you did on page 11.
- Go back to the front mask. Glue the top of a stick to each door.

When you put on your mask, you can use the sticks to open the doors and show the animal behind.

This picture shows a mask of a bird that hides behind a mask of a man's face. It is an old Native North American mask and was worn in tribal dances. You could make a mask like this, or you could make a mask of one happy and one sad face.

Tribal mask, Pacific Northwest.

Try out your own ideas. You can add papier-mâché (see page 12) or glue on things to add different textures.

23

Wild beasts

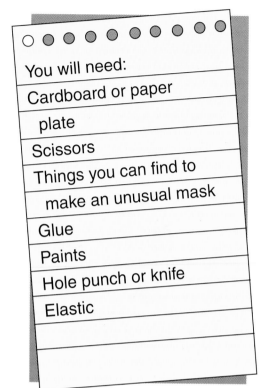

You will need:

Cardboard or paper
  plate
Scissors
Things you can find to
  make an unusual mask
Glue
Paints
Hole punch or knife
Elastic

Masks can be made from almost anything. This picture shows what one artist did with an old bicycle seat and some handlebars.

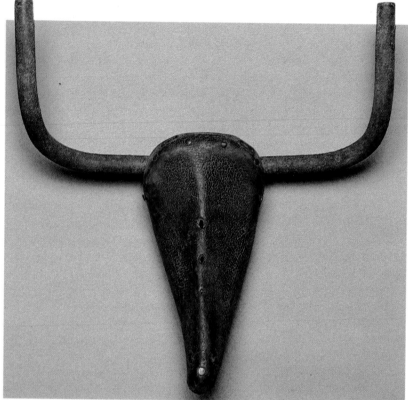

Bull's Head 1942 by Pablo Picasso (1881-1973).

Collect lots of things you could use to make an interesting mask. Look around your home. Then see what else you can find outside. Collect things like cardboard tubes, empty yogurt cups, egg cartons, corrugated cardboard, bottle caps, tree bark, sticks, feathers, and dried leaves.

Look at all your finds and think about what sort of mask you can make.

Use a paper plate as your mask shape or cut a big face shape out of cardboard. Now glue on your found objects. Make interesting textures and patterns. Keep gluing things down until you have something really wild and exciting. Use paints, too.

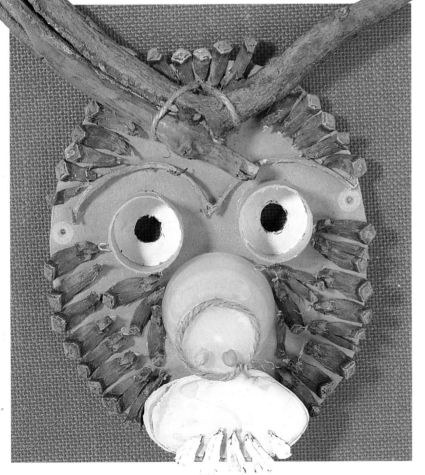

If your mask is not too heavy to wear, make holes for your eyes and add some elastic (see page 11). If it is heavy, hang it on the wall instead.

So far, the masks in this book have been done by looking at the front of a face, so that you see the whole face. What does a face look like from the side? A face seen from the side is called a profile.

You will need:

Cardboard

Pencil

Scissors

Glue

Hole punch

Paints

Elastic

Portrait of Dora Maar by Pablo Picasso (1881-1973).

Look at this painting. Can you see a picture of a face seen from the front as well as from the side?

You can make a mask like this.

● On one piece of cardboard draw a face from the front. Draw a friend or a member of your family. Make it big.

On another piece of cardboard draw the same person's face from the side. Look carefully at the person's profile. You can see only one eye. What does it look like? Cut out both faces, and cut away the back of the head on the profile drawing. Now place the profile on top of the other face and move them around until you like the way they look. Glue them together.

- Paint your mask with bright colors.
- Make holes for your eyes and add elastic (see page 11).

27

Chinese dragons

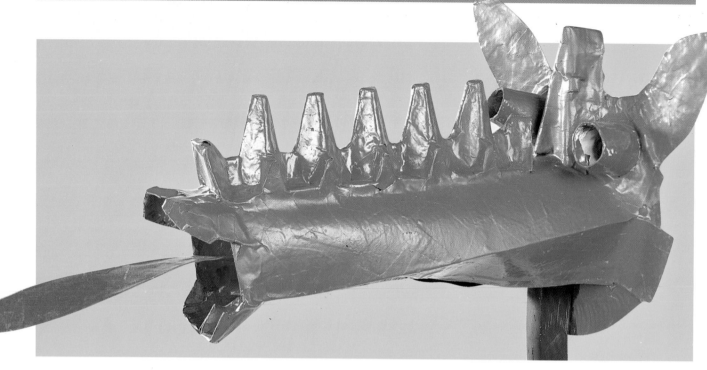

You will need:

Paper plate

Cardboard

Pencil

Scissors

Glue

Paints

A variety of things you can find to make interesting masks, such as egg cartons, cereal boxes, pieces of fabric and yarn, tinfoil

An old sheet (ask an adult for this)

This dragon's head was made with egg cartons, a cereal box, a paper plate, and some cardboard.

Think of your own ideas for masks. Look around you and at pictures in books and magazines. Almost anything can be the beginning for a really exciting mask.

Think about what you can find to use. Everyday objects look very different when they have been painted or have been added to.

This colorful dragon twists and turns through the streets during Chinese New Year celebrations.

Get together with some friends and make a giant creature mask. You can use some of the ideas in this book to help.

Chinese New Year, London, England.

Ask an adult if you can have an old sheet. Paint the sheet or add pieces of fabric and other things to make the creature's body. One person wears the mask while the others stand behind in a row – covered with the sheet – and wriggle around like a monster's back.

Helpful hints

To make a great mask, you don't need fancy equipment or materials. You do need a bold idea. Try to think of something that will make your mask different from others that you've seen. Maybe you will make an unusual face shape. Maybe you will paint your mask with odd patterns or colors. Maybe you will cover your mask with macaroni! Have fun and don't be afraid to try something different.

Here are some helpful hints:

- Keep your mask-making tools in a cardboard carton so everything will be ready when you need it. Keep smaller items, such as buttons or feathers, in an old fish tackle box or shoe box.

- Always spread newspaper over your work surface. Clean up when you are finished so that people won't get upset next time you want to work on a mask.

- Once you have an idea you like, make a few test drawings on paper. First, draw an oval that's about as big as the mask you'll eventually make. If you like the shape, draw over it with a marker, so when you erase mistakes later, the face outline will remain. Lightly sketch in the eyes, nose, and mouth. (Remember that the eyes are about halfway down the face.) Next, pencil in the outline of your design. Once your design outline pleases you, color it in with crayons, markers, paints, pastels, or anything that lets you see how the colors will look. If you don't like the first color combination you come up with, trace the design outline onto another piece of paper and try again.

- Always let your papier-mâché dry before you paint it. A little bit of patience will really pay off with papier-mâché .

- Use your masks to put on a show for your friends. You can make simple costumes. A shirt and pants of the same color might look good, and so would a leotard with a T-shirt.

- Ask a friend to make a mask with you.

Glossary

Actor A person who pretends to be someone or something else in a play.

Camouflage A color or pattern that matches its surroundings. A camouflaged person or animal is difficult to see.

Cave people People who lived in caves thousands of years ago.

Crops Plants that are grown by people, usually to eat.

Elastic A stretchy thread.

Festivals Special days or times of the year when people celebrate something.

Hole punch A special tool for making holes in paper.

Modeling Shaping something out of a soft material, such as clay or modeling compound.

Paper fasteners Pins with two ends. When the pin is pushed through something, the two ends are bent backward to hold the pin in place.

Profile The shape of a face seen from the side.

Self-portrait A picture of oneself.

Texture The feel or look of a surface.

White glue A water based glue.

Further information

Further reading

Gelber, Carol. *Masks Tell Stories*. Beyond Museum Walls. Brookfield, CT: Millbrook Press, 1993.

Green, Jen. *Making Masks and Crazy Faces*. Why Throw It Away? New York: Gloucester Press, 1992.

Morris, Ting and Morris, Neil. *Masks*. Sticky Fingers. New York: Franklin Watts, 1993.

Pryor, Nick. *Putting on a Play*. New York: Thomson Learning, 1994.

Robson, Denny. *Masks and Funny Faces: Activities and Projects*. Rainy Days. New York: Gloucester Press, 1992.

Russon, Jacqueline. *Face Painting*. New York: Thomson Learning, 1994.

Index

animals 18-19, 22-23, 24
birds 20-21, 23
bread dough 16-17
cartoons 12-13
clowns 6
eyeholes 5
faces 4, 6-7, 8, 10, 14-15, 23, 25, 26-27
festivals 4, 29
glasses 8-9

hair 7, 12
hats 13
masks, history of 4
mosaics 10-11
Native Americans 20, 23
papier-mâché 12-13, 14-15, 23
self-portraits 14-15
wearing masks 11

Acknowledgments

The publishers wish to thank the following for the use of photographs:
Robert Harding Picture Library for p. 4 Tassili rock painting, Algeria © F. Jackson and p. 29 Chinese New Year, London, England © Adam Woolfit.
Eye Ubiquitous for p. 5 Masks © Geoff Redmayne; p. 6 (top left) Aborigine from Kakadu, Australia © Matthew McKee and p. 6 (top middle) Chinese opera performer © Julia Waterlow.
Reproduced by kind permission of Christie's Images, p. 16 Tlingit tribal mask.
© The British Museum, London for p. 20 Nishga bird mask and p. 23 Tribal mask.
The Bridgeman Art Library, London for p. 22 *The Dream*, Henri Rousseau © Museum of Modern Art, New York and p. 26 *Portrait of Dora Maar* by Pablo Picasso © DACS 1994.
Musée Picasso, Paris for p. 24 *Bull's Head* 1942 by Pablo Picasso © DACS 1994.
Badger p. 18 by Bridget Sherlock.
All other photographs © Chris Fairclough Colour Library.

The publishers also wish to thank our models Jack, Sophie, Manlai, and Kerry, and our young artists Harry, Sophie, and Jack.